D0862638

Ocean Drinker

Ocean Drinker

New & Selected Poems

Carl Little

DEERBROOK EDITIONS

PUBLISHED BY
Deerbrook Editions
P.O. Box 542
Cumberland, Maine 04021-0542

FIRST EDITION

ISBN: 0-9712488-5-0

On the Cover:
The Wise Man Agastya Represented as Drinker of Ocean
High Punjab, Mandi
Circa 1630-1645
Gouache heightened with gold on paper
Reproduced with permission of
F. Lugt Collection,
Fondation Custodia, Paris, France

Manufactured by Sheridan Books

Cover and book design by Jeffrey Haste

For my families (from whence all verses flow)

and in memory of James Edward Hope (1954-1973)

I recall the morning we awoke
with campfire sunk in snow.
You went to gather tinder;
at your return, my 'thetic joke:
"Eddy, I'd lost all hope."
Where's the sleeping bag that held
the smell of pine and smoke?

Contents

Running Out of Ideas One Day

For dinner, vacation, carnality,
I took up an ancient text on military strategy,
hoping to find the miracle subterfuge,
the perfect pineapple. Instead,

I read how Sanmicheli, inventor
of the "bastion triangular," united
force and elegance in his castles.
Force and elegance—the architecture

of my personal stronghold
has always called for a blank demeanor,
with steep walls and a moat
where crocs and anacondas cruise.

Let the drawbridge down for the shepherd,
for the raiser of geese.
Let the taxman wait in the rain,
his hands softening for want.

I

"There will be no going back."

—May Sarton, "April in Maine"

Heron on the Dam

The cormorant across the water first catches the eye,
crescent wings held open to wind and sun—
perfect feathered cruciform—

then a slender shape off to the right
asserts itself like a statue
suddenly spied in a niched garden of the wealthy,
the perfect blend, like the tobacco mix
my grandfather sought in Amsterdam,

but the heron's gray, his thin legs a miracle
holding him against the flow, and I turn

to look after my son—all this is taking place
in the middle of a perfect New England village—
and note how leaves on the millpond have formed
an exact map of Surinam, where tobacco is harvested,
then shipped to Holland, where my grandfather
inspects it, before sending it on to Virginia

from whence it enters our feeble American lungs,
troubled enough by this perfect Maine air
we're always hearing about, gilded today,

not like lilies, but like the light
in Old Master renderings of the Annunciation,
the dove flying in nonstop on glory rays.

My son tugs at me, and the heron makes a perfect
one-hop take-off, not disturbing a soul,
not even the cormorant, drying in the sunset,

as dark and radiant and perfect
as Christ forgotten on his perch on Calvary.

When I Think of Elvers

I think of the self,
of the eel in me,
the glass eels in all of us,

and I think of Presley
at Graceland, his hips
wriggling into the hearts

women opened to him, fragile,
like the fyke nets that lead
tiny elvers into ice boxes

marked "Japan" where raw fish
slips down eager throats,
salty stuff from the Maine Gulf,

forty bucks a pound for eels
that otherwise would end up
in Somes Pond's muddy bottom,

food for something bigger, 'cause
there's a chain, at the top of which
we stand, skin shiny with sweat,

the effort of the harvest,
making our elver living,
our lives tied to muslin nets

drying in the spring sun
along the banks by the library
where books are free for the taking,

like these transparencies called elvers,
"a variant of *eelfare*, 'the passage
of young eels up a river,'"

or a stream as silver as this one,
filling pockets on the tides,
in the moonlight, slipping

through my fingers in the bad dream
I sometimes have of eels,
of Elvis and of selfish, selfish me.

Ahab on a Whale Watch

One man had the nerve
to ask about my wooden leg;
I turned away with a hiss
and heard the camera's click
capture my lower half.

A guide goes on and on about whale song,
plays it over the intercom
till I boil in my skin—
can't they hear the high-pitched laughter
through all that liquid static?

I shudder at the cheers
when a puny fish, a minke,
breaks water a quarter mile away
and all on board aim lenses
at an empty sea.

My harpoon arm twitches.
I go down below for bad coffee,
the only pair of eyes on this fools' ship
turned inward till
you can see the whites.

At the Touch Tank
(Mount Desert Island Biological Laboratory)

Jake, age six, plunges his arms
into pumped seawater
up to his elbows to wrestle a dogfish,
small shark whose eyes bulge.

On the bottom, tankmates,
skates skim like magic carpets.
Suddenly one of them pops up,
its odd mouth

working in a way
to suggest a talkative thing,
anxious to communicate
yet voiceless.

Pushing through the kids
I lean to touch the skate's skin,
feel a shock, withdraw
my hand as fast

as the fish wings away—
like the first time
I went further than necking
and backed off, not slapped,

but in awe of the sensation
of something encountered
in the dark of a parked car,
nothing I'd ever seen

except in pictures
found at the town dump.
"The skate and the dogfish
do not mate," replies

the biologist on duty
to a little girl's inquiry.
I blush, turn away to study
other sea creatures,

urchins, alewives, fingerlings.

The Lobster

Lobster, pasha of the sea,
lobster blue and lobster red.
Lobster, swimmer in reverse,
if you move , you stir your bed.

Lobster, hermit of rocks,
bad boy, prince without a flaw.
Lobster, glory of markets,
lobster, Lord of the Claw.

(from the French of Robert Desnos)

A Special Intelligence (The Scallop Diver)

Marine biologists look so long at the surface of the sea for
signs
they are able, after years of sweeping eyes over whitecaps,

to distinguish roil of dolphin from wake of wave, to pick
out fin
in sullen ocean, whale exhalation on an overcast day at a
great distance.

This visual acuity represents a special intelligence, to make
out
slightest disturbance, differentiate shades of gray. The
same goes

for those who spend their lives underwater, who discern
scorpion fish
camouflaged amid coral or indentation in the sand that is
flounder,

skate or sole. And the veteran diver who harvests those
shells
whose insides drive diners crazy possessed that sharp
eyesight

that spies fan-shaped mollusks on the Sound's murky
bottom,
but chill water numbed his head and air from the sixth
tank ran thin

and ice made an extra curtain to block dull winter light,
and in panic
the diving man inflated the suit and felt his torso expand
as if he were

The Incredible Hulk, and he soared like Superman over
tall buildings
to bump against the terrible canopy that held him under
like a mean cousin,

drowning him yards from his boat and sternman who
                                        waited a while before
getting scared and radioing the Coast Guard, and the
                                        coxswain trained

to find people lost at sea, to pick out bodies in the surf, to
                                        peer through
thickest fog, spotted the body among broken ice and had
                                        the awful honor

to haul in the heavy human catch survived by four
                                        children and a mother.
O, diver lost beneath the ice: darkness overcomes us all at
                                        end of day.

*For Lewis E. Green, 41, died in Somes Sound, February 6,
1998*

Beachcomber (After the Argument)

Here's the rope that didn't hold,
coiled serpent-like in sea grape,

sandal washed off deck in a gale,
bleach bottle cut in half

to serve as bailer and, further on,
fluorescent light bulb

miraculously whole among coral shards.
And your ex's sunglasses—

remember the scene on the dock
when you sent them winging?

Beyond the reef are wrecks,
but the tide line offers its own

special treasures: a vial
of yellow liquid, a glass buoy

and enough timber in one stretch
to build yourself a hut whose walls

you'd decorate with sea fans
and colored glass, and earn

a living sketching black men
splitting langouste by the pier,

with spare time given to trying
to make sense of detritus:

Through whose hair ran this calcified brush?
What child lost the pink snorkel,

purple pail without handle?
Which sailboat is missing a bar set?

And who was the liar who declared
so many centuries ago that

distant shores held promise?

Notes from Hilton Head

Chihuly jellyfish, hundreds of them
(if they were actual glass we'd be talking
exhibition at the new aquarium in Charleston)
strewn across flats where bikers
riding low-slung three-wheelers whip along
like Roman charioteers on vacation.

Ticky-tacky mansions confuse you.
Flat sea, straight horizon, huge balls
in a thong. You see a
need for more effective signage:
For ecological reasons,
stay the fuck off the dunes!

Wildlife adapts, birds
nesting in topiary hedges,
'gators hanging out
in golf course canals,
hired carps Hoovering
brown pools between sundecks.

A heron snags a fish,
the shape visible in its throat.
Your golfing partner says,
"That's nasty."
Not nasty, pal, it's
tasty and hyper Japanese.

Swimming Head

> "Fishermen's children would bind chunks of sun
> fish skin with twine to form bouncy balls."
> --Tierney Thys, *Natural History*

What the Germans call *schwimmenderkopf*,
"swimming head," because that's what it seems to be,
a fish that is all head, poor thing,
the ocean sunfish waved a palsied fin
at the watchers who'd come for whales,
but who craned over the railing
to keep in their sights this odd creature,
huge yet hardly leviathan, making its aimless way
within the upper reaches of deep sea

waving that weak fin all the while
like the tortured end of a thalidomide arm
at the staring crowd who were themselves
green at the gills from racing over the waves
in search of finbacks and minkes,
which never appeared, not even
an exhalation on the horizon, nothing
to hail with a lusty "thar she blows,"

only this fish seemingly all alone out in the ocean,
as if it were the last surviving swimming thing,
trundling its pale body off the starboard side,
weakly waving, named *mola* by Linnaeus
after its millstone shape, heaviest
of all bony fishes (as much as
5,000 pounds the marine scientists say),
spooky, sun-worshipping, out of luck on this

overcast Gulf of Maine day, and doomed
if some sportive sea lions should appear—
unlikely here—and toss it about like a Frisbee
(we read of this dreadful possibility
in *Natural History*), fated anyway
to lose its audience as the spectators

leave off their looking one by one,
and the boat veers off, carving waves,
its captain hoping to scare up whales,

while up on deck one gentleman keeps talking
about the sunfish, how he watched sharks
take chunks out of one, turning gray wave to red,
during his last solo Atlantic crossing, how
they lack magnificence despite their size,
and only a young woman disagrees and
holds her infant child in her arms
and glares at the Hemingway wannabe,

remembering how she kept sight of that head
in the sea, bodiless, till it was beyond view,
and the way she felt impelled to wave goodbye,
which she now regrets as a melodramatic gesture
and how, for consolation, her mind's eye shifted
to other sunfish, the freshwater kind,
sweeping their nests by the dock
in early June on Long Island, gasping

when pulled from the pond by thoughtless children,
gills fluttering in the terrible air.
"They can't be kin," she thinks, and dismisses
the old man of the sea who would scoff
at her sentiments, however genuine they might be.
She promises to teach her child
the wonders of sunfish great and small
and to cheer for the kingdom of the sea.

**"Bathing Suit, ca.1900, believed to have belonged
to Rachel Field of Sutton Island"** *(Northeast Harbor Collection)*

Your last name stitched to the collar
like mine when sent off
to tennis camp.
Your bathing suit, better called
a dress, tacked to a door

at an angle, ragged,
but with nifty striped
belt, collar, hem.
Your name imprinted in my head,
poet who "once slept

on an island,"
who died way too young
in alien California,
who resurrected Captain Samuel Hadlock, Jr.,
his luck, his curse,

the final pocket—
God's, you called it—
in the Greenland ice
where Cranberry Island shipmates
let slip his frozen body.

Did you wear this suit
to take the chill waters
of Sutton Island?
I touch it surreptitiously, hoping
for the electricity that runs

through history and clothes,
in this room of artifacts,
upstairs from the player piano
that just happens to be pounding out
Beautiful Dreamer.

A Reminder (Great Cranberry Island)

It is one sort of evidence of living:
         a wash hung in the yard
between the house and a tree or some such
         arrangement for holding things
off the ground. Sheets snap like sails,
         a bra trails a strap, its
guard let down. An only shirt (tropical
         fish pattern) flutters about
till its arms entangle or go limp for
         want of wind. What's dry

gets taken in before the dusk dampens it,
         the vacation over so to speak.
Once more a faded yellow towel will fold
         neatly in three or someone's
favorite pants be re-mended. Crisp linen
         may twist beneath lovers
excited to old desires by the freshness
         upon which they lie.
And as one supposes every household has

         its weakness, so each home
the length of this island has a wash.
         But of certain things
one must be, from time to time, reminded:
         happiness, for instance,
mortality, and even (and this is my argument)
         that wide assortment
of odd clothing that droops in the dark,
         forgotten tonight, haunting
the house to which we are all attached
         by a good strong cord.

for William Kienbusch, 1914-1980

Young Pine

The white pine that happened to grow
needles-to-clapboard at the back of the shed
looks like it is hiding

from the cops or a gang
or is simply playing hide-and-seek,
a nine-year-old girl, say,

with gentle boughs
hugging the corner of the outbuilding,
trembling in a breeze, hoping

no one notices her until
she can reach a size where the house owner
won't consider her

spindly enough to be cut down.
Lithe, small, hidden,
the young pine is beautiful.

Someone should embrace her
as she grows toward the roofline,
save her from the saw.

Ten Tourists Visit Baker's Island, Maine, ca. 1900

Mason:
This hurly-burly, these misshapen slabs,
I can barely stomach it, yet
what walls I could make.

Dancer:
These pink platforms by the sea!
Where is my partner?
Where are my slippers?

Aquarellist:
Hues, here, by the score,
the sea calling for blues,
the sky washing the horizon.

College Professor:
I catch my thoughts between
sea beats and find Blake
in a grain of granite.

Geologist:
I have died and gone to heaven!
Oh, heart swollen by stone!
Oh, ledge of eternity!

Mortician:
Boulders mock the symmetry
of chiseled graveyard markers—no
monument in this place.

Naturist:
Skin warmed by rock,
I lie in my hidden alcove,
chapel for sun worship.

Composer:
The sounds are chaotic
Where surf slams the isle—
notations for a sea symphony.

Natural Historian:
Only I notice rafts of eider
in ocean hollows, and tide pools
reveal whole worlds.

Stowaway:
I explore the glorious edge
as the boat full of fools
sails back to the mainland.

"3,000 Dreams Explained"

Early in the course of a night's dreaming
I smoke a cigarette, which may mean
success of one sort or another.
Later, around dawn, I ride bareback
alongside my brother through water.
Horses imply independence in the future;
I don't recall their color,
but white and black can signify
a wedding and death,
respectively. At last
we stumble upon an island,
according to my handbook loneliness to come.

I toss the guide aside
to work my own interpretations.
Wasn't David about to join me
in a house off the coast of Maine?
And wouldn't there be horses
in the mailboat's engines carrying us across?
Without Madame Aspasia's assistance
I relive the thrill of last night's episodes:
a bad habit of the past embraced again,
and my brother and I, complete strangers
to riding, whipping our steeds
up out of the frigid waters.

Whirligig

Compelled by coastal breeze, gust,
full-fledged wind, the sawyer
works the toothless band across the log,
cutting nothing.
There's something existential
in his labor, yet the balding artisan
shows no sign of frustration, anger, terror.
Even when the air stills, the man of wood
remains intent on his impossible task,
slightly bent over the saw—a stance
to set a chiropractor smiling.

Symbol of some ideal work ethic
he is not. The gentleman
who crafted him simply wished
to give pleasure to the eye—
the figure is brightly hued—
and the ear: in a wind
the contraption makes a lovely light clatter
akin to a loved one's laughter
at the gift of a well-chosen bracelet.

A toast, then, to this man-on-a-stick,
swiveling without effort in the evening air,
and let's raise a glass
to the carpenter on Mullein Hill
who cut this carpenter out of wood,
whirligig that time and again
fulfills the aspirations of the wind.

to the memory of Arthur and Phyllis Charpentier

Ocean Drinker

(After an anonymous Indian painting)

Whereas the wise Agastya
sits cross-legged on a deerskin,
drinking up the water before him
with his eyes closed
like someone returning to the coast
after a bad winter inland, who
inhales the first lungful
of sea air with no need
to view the watery plain
somewhere beyond a stone wall, a privet hedge;

whereas the wise man shares his grassy lot
with small deer, quail, a peacock
and a few tall trees that stand out
against the blue evening sky;
whereas there's a second figure, to
Agastya's right, who waits to have a word
with wisdom itself,
who watches the bearded figure
take up the flourishing, linear seas
into his thin body with no
apparent toil or perturbation;

whereas other oceans
remain to be cleansed,
I cling ever tighter to the notion
of discarding calm.
For were I to settle on some promontory
jutting out into the Atlantic,
I couldn't appreciate the wide waters
in the all-encompassing manner
of Agastya, who obliges
student or cousin or creditor
to keep a respectful distance.

And even if it were my will to take up
a contemplative position,
to reduce my possessions to a hide,

a string of beads and something
to tie back my long hair—
to turn inward, hauling nature
after me—I would not forsake
a tiny daughter dressed in red
breathing a soft whisper
in her sleep, abandon
the wiles and landmarks of my wife,

not leave off my travels now,
today, to become another beacon
on some desolate point,
helpful now and again,
photogenic, yet
no more in the end
than a big eye whose beam
glances off treacherous waters,
doesn't take them in

and fails entirely before the fog.

Closing the House (Great Cranberry)

Each bayonet of goldenrod
bears witness to the sun's final flare
before the cold sets in.

The single backyard apple tree
will remain a good home for worms,
its wizened fruit, gathered

by tenants, dropping a faint stain
on a sill. The cellar door
slopes up to a first floor window

where the boy who cuts the lawn
happened upon a lovely view:
breasts grazed by a pair

of long hands just as
the mid-afternoon sunlight
touched the sofa bed.

This house will hold its breath
through winter, then bare again
its floors to strangers.

II

"World well broken. Shack on a reef."

—Joseph Donahue

"Death Toll Rises to More Than 500 in Liberian Massacre" *(Photo: Agence France-Presse)*

They appear to be asleep,
but the *New York Times* doesn't give front-page space
to a photograph of two women and two children sleeping,
even if they sleep in the road.

One child rests its head on the lower back
of one of the women—no, its head
rests on the woman, the child's life
has been taken. The second youngster shares

its mother's skirt; the way
they lie so close to each other,
the small arm circling the large arm,
you feel comfort, although the woman's face

presses flat into the ground
and her left wrist twists unnaturally.
They could be taking an afternoon nap,
these Liberians lying in the dust,

but the *New York Times* doesn't give
front page space to a photograph
of Liberians napping, even if they
happen to be napping in the middle of a road.

Somes Harbor (February 2003)

Ice splits into continents
illustrating plate tectonics
floes breaking into countries
that divide in turn like the Balkans—
here Serbia, there Bosnia—
but wind- , not war-torn.

Weeding Roses (The War)

Crowding each other in July peak
Rosa rugosa lift blossoms
over sills so their aroma
enters the kitchen when windows
are opened for air. In shorts,

MOFGA tee shirt, no gloves,
I'm a glutton for thorns
(some remain embedded for weeks
like reporters in Iraq).
How many times have I gone

through these motions?
Grip at base of weed, careful tug
to loosen roots, then yank
and fling. Mother, father,
you're the ones who set me

on this mission years ago
to rid the world of invasive plants.
Famous nowadays for clothes
strewn on bedroom floor,
bureau top that might be

a midden, I'll have you know
your second son loves more
than most things in this life
the sight of roses free of weeds,
the sight of soldiers coming home.

His Letters

All summer the word "love"
scythed in the tall meadow grass
angered his wife. On her walks
with the dog, she avoided it,
threatening to have a gardener
mow it down for mulch.

He thought the word "love"
scythed in the tall meadow grass
would please his children
who disliked war, even
the war he'd fought in.
They told him it was nice,

but told each other the word "love"
scythed in the tall meadow grass
wouldn't do. He kept it trim,
hoping someone might search him out
from the air, come stepping
from the woods, a woman

who'd say the word "love"
scythed in the tall meadow grass
made her lose her head.
His letters bow low
to the first frost, no skirt
snagged in the knee-high thistles.

Desire Lines

They are the paths worn across lawns,
unofficial thoroughfares,
"the people's choice."

They are the lyrics in a poem or song, "Shall I
compare thee to a summer's night" or "I wanna be
your lover, baby, I wanna be your man."

They are invisible midway points in the bed
that we cross over in our sleep,
seeking heat.

They are different from sites of opportunity and
constraint. They are where we want to go
on our walks to the other side of campus,

in our arts, in our half-waking state.

for Millard Dority

Glacial Erotic

When the great sheet of ice retracted,
enormous boulders were left scattered
on mountainsides and deep in forests.
They assumed unusual positions.

One massive example, with smooth top
and curved sides, served as the trysting place
for lovers from the town of Bar Harbor.
They assumed unusual positions.

You say erratic, I say erotic, let's call
the whole thing rock. And when the glaciers
next return, flipping us over in our beds,
we, too, will assume most unusual positions.

Car on a Lift

Nearer my god to thee.

Whee, this is fun,
lifted hydraulically.
What a weight
off my radials,
I didn't realize how
exhausted I was.
Heaven looks like
the upper reaches
of Midas in Ellsworth.
I muffle my sobs (I
am a Saab)
of pleasure.
Leave me here, suspended,
if but for an hour
of elevation.
I am high on life
already, the new muffler
will be a bonus.
Heights don't scare me,
I'm red and a 9000
and could easily get used
to this lofty perch,
the smell of the grease,
the roar of the engines.

Muse on I-95 (September)

This highway would seem like the last place
you'd find her, yet here she is, offering images:
osprey nest atop a telephone pole, contingent
of weeping willows in the median, the words
"Palmyra, Next Right," spire on a distant hill,
tall grass among a stand of pines, a farm, a field,
a single birch like a lightning bolt among spruce,
G.O.D. (Guaranteed Overnight Delivery) on a truck,
camper with Florida plates heading out of state,
out-of-season snowplow, shipment of golf carts,
and a girl, my lord, in a flatbed Ford, slowing down
for construction work just this side of Waterville.

Frost Heaves

The oysters didn't sit well
in the belly
of the bard,
and the end-of-winter
roller-coaster roads
didn't help
matters.

Frost heaves,
gets back into the car,
adjusts his scarf,
wondering whose woods these are
where he just barfed.

To the Lady Who Sets Out Lawn Ornaments Every Morning

Alpha leader, how lost
in thought you seem, placing
black silhouettes of dogs
wearing neck bandannas
across the grass, arranging
Canada geese in a comely flock
that fools a few folks driving by,
yours an art of proper placement,
the right number of figurines,
not too many Tweety Birds.
Trolls regard mini lighthouses and
whirligigs make a fine racket
along the route after a truck
goes rushing by toward Bar Harbor.
Cars distort in blue glass globes
reminding you of mirrors at the fair
that thin you down to nothing.
A little black bear clinging
to a post is your favorite, not
because the animal's so cunnin'
but because you can relate
to a creature holding on
for dear life every day.

Self-Storage (North Anson, Maine)

> "A lot of storage is emotional."
> --Mary Ann Solet, *Ellsworth Weekly*

"They're poppin' up all over,"
says a lady awaiting soft serve, guiding
your eyes to dull structures nearby.

Behind blank portals lie
excess inventory, furnishings,
items that never sell at yard sales

yet can't be thrown away,
family heirlooms that threatened
to evict you, stacks of paper

requiring a lawyer's review
when the case makes it to court.
The self gets stored there, too,

behind folding garage doors
painted a shade of beige on sale
year-round at the hardware store.

If you could rent a self-storage unit
with a dairy bar on one side,
a weigh station on the other

and an intermodal facility
somewhere close by, you'd be
a fulfilled human being, you think,

licking your cone furiously.

For Linden Frederick

Self Claim Area (LaGuardia)

Whitman passing through security,
musing aloud, "I salute
the hunkering humankind
crowding into airplanes,
I admire the uniformed man
running the squeaking wand
up and down my pantlegs."
What a broad smile he wears,
hat in hand, claiming himself
on the far side of the detector.

Double the Size of Your Schlong

When one Freddy Puckett asks
":Wa'nt a ^ big D;ICK?"
I'm not in the least taken aback
by the random punctuation
in his spam. He deploys
colons, apostrophes and the like
with the verve of a guy
with a foot-long and balls
like okra jars. My schlong,
God bless it, if it could speak
would probably give the okay
to enlargement pills and
growth oils—delusions of
grand girth and long length—
heed the surreal subject line
"stick this plaster & see ur peni-s
grow sliced flowerless" or the
urgent "SIZE MATTERS!"
Or maybe it would read the question
"Still no luck enlarging it?"
hang its head in shame,
or send a dark stare my way
as if somehow it were my fault
that it hasn't grown for years
despite the stretching exercises.
My penis, my companion,
I beg your forgiveness.
Let's hang for a while and see
what the next email brings.

Cardiac Infarction

What bold "r"s these words can brag,
so much stronger than those
offered by red scare or Aryan race.

Cardiac has a lot of heart;
infarction arrests it in its tracks.

Ring for the gurney, the cart,
the doctor to fibrillate the organ
from whence all internal roads—
some called arteries—

start. You can't ignore
those hard "r"s, bolder than
Horn & Hardart.

Possible Last Suppers

It's true death row inmates get to select
whatever they desire for the ultimate meal—
boeuf bourguignon with Chateau Lafitte,
shrimp gumbo, a pan of manicotti.

Asked what she'd order for her last repast,
Julia Child replied with a full menu
including "foie gras, oysters and a little caviar
to begin with . . . , [then pan-roasted duck]

accompanied by little onions,
chanterelle mushrooms and little potatoes,
with a sauce made out of the carcass."
Your son, you think, might choose

pepperoni pizza, your daughter,
a Carnation instant mocha milk shake,
plus angel hair pasta; a fondue
for your wife. Given the choice,

you'd ask the waiter/jailer for
a large plate of Swedish meatballs,
a joint smoked beforehand
spiking the appetite.

Any meal might be your last.
Christ, you hope you don't croak
following this lunch
of leftover chop.

III

Having and giving but also catching glimpses
hints that are revelations: to have been so happy is a promise
and if it isn't kept that doesn't matter. It may snow
falling softly on lashes of eyes you love and a cold cheek
grow warm next to your own in hushed dark familial
December.

—James Schuyler, "December"

Somesville Invitation

The gently sloping Japanese bridge
is hard to resist, from any angle.
Today the arc and its reflection

in slightly filmy water
form a long oval of invitation,
like an odd-shaped mirror glimpsed

through piled furniture at an auction—
an opening to another world.
Leaning over the rail my daughter and I

can see what we'd find: a brown streambed
with weeds bent by the flow; no fish;
ducks pursuing their food search

in the reeds. It's true we're all looking
for something, in the woods, in water,
under sofa cushions; call it

the glint of good fortune. Meanwhile
bridges help us get over things
or simply provide a shortcut to school.

Emily wants to traverse the ice-creaky planks
again and again, hoping for magic,
trolls and the like, but I tell her,

wisely I think, that we've got to get
to know this stream-leaper a lot better
before we can expect such wonders.

Yet this temptation in the landscape
already has us where it wants:
helpless and heartened in its narrow hold.

A Family of Four Acts Out "Peter & the Wolf"
(Listening to Leonard Bernstein)

Aprowl, the father wears away
the knees on his best suit
against his wife's scolding.
She wanted to play
the wolf, but accepts
the part of the duck
and also that of the grandfather,

waddling and stooping, respectively.
The daughter, in tutu,
flutters about the father's head,
which snaps with conviction.
She is Peter's ally, the bird,
but she also plays Peter
and even acts the cat.

The son bearing imitation Kentucky rifle
refuses to be anything
but one of the hunters, drawing
a bead on his father, though
Bernstein's narrative calls
for shots in the air.
With a flourish, the father-wolf

swallows the mother-duck,
who, as the kindly but gruff grandfather,
warns her daughter, who is Peter,
not to wander beyond the gate.
Now the feline daughter
eyes the bird—herself—
while as Peter she ties a noose

in a jump rope to trap the beast
hungering below the chair,
which represents the tree
whose branches reach over the fence.
There is the click of the fake rifle.
There is the foolish duck

feathering the father's belly.
There is proud Peter exchanging
tutu for pajamas and the wolf
led off through darkening woods
which is the kitchen.
There is the curtain of life.

The Poetry Ken

(for Emily, who thought there ought to be one)

He is not a hunk.
His hair has a lyric unruliness.
He comes with pen, pencil and paper.
His hands are soft, unused
        to work.
He never wears a tux.
He can be melancholy.
He loves "Hawaiian Fun Barbie"
        for her mind.
He hugs trees and speaks to birds.
He dislikes light rock.
His t-shirt reads "Reagan for Fuhrer."
He doesn't use deodorant.
He likes to be called "K."
His chest features hair.
He wants to live with "Benetton Barbie"
        before making a commitment.
He is sensitive.
He's the "Poetry Ken."

Garret sold separately.

The Sculptors

My son and I cast the man's body
out of fresh snow, rolling from the lawn's
periphery to the center three balls
(boulders, really) as tradition calls for.
Mittened hands carve

basic features, scrape out
sections between body parts
like a miracle liposuction,
the snowman based on
no known individual,

finally add generic carrot,
briquettes left over from summer
for eyes (oh, blackest of orbs)
and atop misshapen skull
place a Red Sox batting helmet,

as if this gent will ever don pinstripes....
In the weeks that follow, nature—
wind, rain, sweeping snow—takes over,
so that one day the man hulks
like Rodin's Balzac and the next

assumes the smooth contours
of a Henry Moore sculpture, then
is plastered with needles and looks
vaguely like a George Segal city dweller.
Eventually he slumps forward

as if suffering some ultimate osteoporosis,
becoming minimalist, helmet
fallen from the crooked head
which has lost its features
(a neighbor's horse ate its orange nose),

until, on this late winter day,
the man of snow perishes
in the same sun that warms
our hands where James and I
shag flies in the thawing April yard.

The Gymnasts

Air handlers muffle the commands
of coaches, encouraging
their young charges to make
cleaner dismounts. "Stick
the landing," one of them calls,
and leaps to her feet
to demonstrate how to fly and land
straight as a totem pole,
but less grim. The girls
awaiting their turn

whisper to each other—
it sounds like they're praying
for balance, but it may be
gossip. Gym floors
shine blond with wax.
My daughter, in black,
tiptoes across the beam,
a stretch of polished wood
she badly wants to master.
Boys with basketballs sit
impatient in the bleachers, laughing
too loud for my liking.

Now the split, now the roll,
now the back walkover.
My breathing halts
when Emily sails off
head over heels
and lands—ah!—solid
on the blue square of mat.
Later, orange soda in hand,
she will bubble on about
how close she and her friends came
to achieving perfection.

Watching the First Pictures from Mars in Logan Airport
While Waiting for a Plane to Bangor, Maine

> "People will do their doctoral theses on this data."
> —CNN Reporter

As the folks at Mars central cheer, as images
of the planet arrive, as the contours of an arid spot
in space are beamed across millions of miles,
as they ooh and aah at the sight of a Martian rock
or are confused for a moment by the edge of an airbag,

my mind wanders to things I would personally like to find
upon landing in an unknown section of the solar system:
a signed photograph of Mickey Mantle, say, or a first
                    edition
of Moby Dick, inscribed by Melville to Nathaniel
                    Hawthorne,
or one of Marilyn Monroe's pillows, still scented.

Oh, but I'm being greedy and what I truly want to
                    discover
is heaven, to know that the place actually exists,
or, better, to come upon a thriving green orb populated by
huge yet harmless iguanas, and snakes with four
                    marvelous heads,
anything but this desolate outpost, dusty and inhospitable,

brought to us by CNN. Mars, where is thy mystery?
The Little Prince would understand my disappointment
at the digital renderings of your barren surface.
And then from my seat in the terminal waiting room
I catch out of the corner of my eye the tail end

of a wonderful sunset and walk to the window to watch
the sun light up the airport, the planes, many of them
                    delayed
on this Independence Day, and think about this fiery glow
striking all of New England, bearing the day's final warmth
to those kind men, women and children who sit on porches

or play catch, blissfully missing history being made.
My daughter and I wait to board the plane to Maine,
                              happy
our craft is not headed to miserable Mars, red planet,
distant, sullen, so much fodder for future Ph.D.s,
but rather north and east to the country of the pointed firs

where the lights of Bangor glint in the darkness,
fireworks bursting over the lost legend of Norumbega,
to our home in the woods and our rooms and our lake
and our son and brother and mother and wife, plus
dog, cat and rabbit, all stayed up late to greet us.

The Man from U.N.C.L.E.

I am not the Man from U.N.C.L.E.,
but Ilya Kuryakin was my hero
in fifth grade, TV Russian-American
wearing turtlenecks
spying for the good guys.
I preferred him to Napoleon Solo—
what a name!—and
planned to enter espionage
after elementary school.

One Christmas I requested a Cold War toy,
a radio that turned into a machine gun
at the push of a button.
Who would suspect a boy
listening to the top forty
might in a flash and
a hail of bullets become
the heart of the party?

Can't recall what the letters U.N.C.L.E.
stand for: University of Nebraska
Cooperative Learning Extension?
I curse my lack
of trivia retention.

My spying days behind me,
now I am an actual uncle
with lots of great nieces and nephews.

for Andrei Codrescu

Tying His Son's Tie

He's a public schooler unlike his elitist father
who trotted off in uniform every morning and
he's taller than his sire, who goes on tiptoe

to peer over shoulder and reach around neck
to tie the tie, fingers fumbling, though
he has maneuvered these strips of cloth

a thousand times at least—daily noose
of business wear. The father recalls lines
from a childhood song, *I'm dressing myself,*

what have I here? These are your
socky, socks, socks, my darling dear,
and how he and his siblings rolled

on the rug when the goofy singer reached
the point where the child puts on his *underpants,*
pants, pants in front of his proud mother.

Proud father walks around handsome son
to tug the tie into place, fix the collar,
admire the height the boy now soars to,

speak reassuring words as they prepare
to cross the island to the service for a friend
lost forever on a mountain in Maine.

In memory of Pam Fountain (1952-2003)

Tiger Woods PGA Tour 2004 (The Game)

Computer game in a pause mode
I watch Woods approach the tee,
address the ball, tug
at the left shoulder of his shirt,
settle in, line up his drive,
then step back, with a look

of concern: something keeps him
from swinging. Turning his back
to me, Tiger surveys the sweep
of gorgeous virtual fairway,
raising a five iron to his chest
like a knight, then returns

to the task at hand, perfected
ritual: sleeve tug, slight
settling shuffle, stiffening
of composure and resolve,
interrupted once again by
awareness he can't proceed.

In a trance I watch him for a while,
feeling bitter about his situation
and mine, about desires denied—
another year not climbing Katahdin,
another missed mission to Ecuador—
all the personal hooks and slices

landing in rough way left, way right.
I reach for the keyboard, unwilling
to let the golfer suffer anymore,
click "quit," as if that directive
will do the trick for either of us
stuck in a limbo of half swings.

for James, who left it on

68

Winter Olympics Revisited

Jumping back and forth
between this poem
and a game
of computer solitaire,
my vagrant thoughts are further
interrupted by
sharp intakes of breath,
my wife in the next room watching
figure skaters who
circle, spin, leap, twirl and
sometimes fall,
the latter causing
those gasps
I associate with
Chiller Theater,
the tax bill
and estimates on Antiques Roadshow.

Red Nightshirt

A flawless field appears, prime
for planting, where seeds sown one day
provide a harvest the next,
where weather always accommodates
and your kids eat all their vegetables.

Or an occasion for renewal and repose
presents itself, melancholy diverted
like a muddy stream through
a bright new aluminum culvert
lowered by crane. Then there's the dream

of sorting things out, in which
every bead from a broken necklace
rolls out from under the radiator,
pops up from a crack in the floor
into your deft fingers.

Meeting up with your best old buddy
you will save him from a knifing
or simply communicate without words.
And if you happen to be sporting
a red nightshirt (as I am),

when at last you touch base
with the sleepy depths
you'll come into a small fortune
of rare books with unheard-of literary associations,
or, better still, be implicated

in a warm conspiracy
to help the poor, comfort
your daughter with wondrous words,
love your wife beyond restraint.

Springer on Chaise Lounge

Always clambering on,
so we gave up and
covered the chaise
with a faded India print.
We rarely occupied this
furnishing anyway, never
had sex on it (I associate it
with bordellos, hence
this idea). Its bottom

drags on the floor,
straps fixed once tearing again
like poor bandaging.
We would have sunk out of sight
had we tried to maneuver
our bodies atop it, but the
big-for-his-breed Springer
lies in comfort, in
slumber, his eyes rolled up
in his handsome head.

A while back a woman called in
to a radio psyche show
to say she couldn't live
with a pet's death.
I will think of her when I
burn the wounded chair
in the backyard,
watch strands of dirty smoke
slip into the blankety-blank sky.

for Dr. Linda Austin

Snorkeling alongside Buster in Echo Lake

I think of Eadweard Muybridge,
photos he made of a galloping horse
proving four hooves
leave the ground all at once
(for science or to win
a wager, I can't recall).

Springer running through water,
legs steady as a locomotive,
August coat flowing,
beats any Caribbean reef,
except perhaps for the manta
spied one day trailing baby rays

or the sea turtle at Salt Pond Bay.
Flippers allow me to keep up
with spaniel, whose paws
displace water. Awed
by pure motion, I feel voyeuristic
as if seeing something I shouldn't

below the lake's surface,
powerful canine grace, and so
rejoin him in the air and delight
in the light whistle he makes
through his nose and imitate
his paddle as best I can

all the way back to the dock.

IV

"Let's roll this whole movie backwards."

—David Graham

The Facts of Catching

My father ice fishing at night
after his father forbade it
comes up with a pickerel
of record length
and runs
only to fall through
where it's thin,
rushes glinting moonlight
ten feet away
till knees and elbows pull him to shore.

His father, storming
to be wakened so late,
admires the long body
still breathing,
staining the cardboard
on which, by tradition,
the largest fish alone
are outlined,
sketched in, the facts
of their catching
noted underneath:
hour, bait, fisherman.

And I, son and grandson,
attentive to the story's
telling and retelling,
should be listed
as witness, except
I've got it all wrong
I'm told years later:
grandfather was that boy
poorly dressed
for a midwinter's vigil
on forbidden ice.

What's the difference?
I answer back,
to myself:
as long as it's understood
how magnificent fish
get caught, drawn,
handed down;
and how honor
may sometimes follow
a broken word
between son and father,

a shattered pond
freezing over in the background.

The Pickerel

The pickerel makes a lot of plans.
"I'll go see," says he,
"the Ganges and the Nile,
the Tagus and the Tiber,
and the Yangtze River.
I will go, I am free
to make use of my time."

And the moon?
Will you go see the moon?
Pickerel the wayfarer,
pickerel with an evil heart,
fortune-seeking pickerel.

from the French of Robert Desnos

The Longing

I am still waiting for the alligator
my mother sent me from Florida
thirty years ago.

The reptile I had in mind,
but lost in the mail,
fit in a fish bowl, but imagination

allowed the amphibian to outstretch
sink, tub, wading pool until, mid-summer,
he was big enough to ride.

And we go exploring the cold springs
that lead to streams, then a river
flowing by a heron with head

tucked away in a wing, past
turtles sunning on half-sunken timber,
and we head south for the Everglades.

Safely arrived, I am the first person
to learn the secret of their long smiles.
And neither January in its icy ruin

nor a house grown dark in the distance
can keep me from waiting,
warmed by a longing that

bares its teeth and won't let go.

The First Big Hit

The boy clamored to have the record
played again, "It's Istanbul,
Not Constantinople," the two names
tied forever to an age
when he thought nothing
of hearing the same song
three or four times in succession.

Once, following the thumping bass,
his parents made the motions
of a wild dance; he laughed till
tears welled to witness such a marriage
of the familiar and foreign.
The syllables' rolling rhythm
bore the family on through
August 1957, pulsing

from speakers set behind
the sofa where he would crawl
to feel the music with his hands.
Caught up in an Eastern beat,
stretched out on a living room floor:
that's a leisure allowed
children who choose the heart
of a cool, dark house
as a place for travel.

Marie Antoinette

All of eight, present at my first execution
I pale. The hens to an odd jig,
headless and in every direction.
Father consoles:
They're dumber than us, that's all.
Marie Antoinette had the sense to stay put.

One plump matron strews
neck feathers across the yard,
but I am staring at the poor queen
staggering to her feet
to part the gaping crowd,
as the black-hooded man, my father,

runs a rag across the bloody blade.

Moose Head

Shot by Teddy Roosevelt
somewhere in Ontario,
stuffed and shipped
to a New York City men's club,
auctioned to make wall space
for a portrait
of the late president,
the moose—its head—grinned
in the back of the barn,
one of father's Old Golds
stuck between its lips.

One childhood day
with nothing better to do
I went to pry
the moose's marble eyes
with a screwdriver.
But when the ladder
grazed the long face
and ocher dust
puffed from cavernous nostrils,
I stumbled down the rungs
in that dark space
and raced into the light,

remembering a favorite aunt
who'd come to us to die,
how her breathing
yellowed the pillowcase.

Backboard

Built by Freddy, following
father's specs, the board
was the place
to take it all out
and maybe improve your tennis game.
Sometimes the ball sailed over
into the brush or
hit a nailhead and took off
in an unexpected orbit,
yet the pleasure
of pounding, of completing
fifty passable backhands
in a row, more than made up
for the miss-hits.

I skidded across
the HarTru, made
the perfect drop shot,
then sent a rocket down the line.
The dinner bell found me
winning at Wimbleton
or at least taking a set
from my older brother
with his damned uncanny sense
of placement.
Bam, bam, bam, bam—
they gave up on the bell
and called my name,
and I took a few more swipes,
gathered the balls
and headed in.

Cousin Bucko took his fists
to the wall one day,
then broke his racket
in a rage.
Whatever bothered Bucko
didn't get to me:

I smashed the backboard
and held it in highest esteem.

for Frederick Grimshaw

The Clearing

The sunbox lies in pieces,
its strips of aluminum foil
flaking away to the wind,
tanning platform broken up
for kindling. Planted grass
sprouts where the path once
sharply turned to the left
circumventing underbrush,
where the man (a boy then)
stumbled on beauty's wrath:
pale sisters yelling him off,
scrambling for clothes to cover.

All has been cleared, thick
cat briar raked into piles
and set ablaze, invincible
ailanthus stacked for dump.
All's clear and calm save
his childhood rushing head-
long through tearing thickets,
and the sisters, barely glimpsed
against reflective flashing,
laughing after him, then
lying back to catch
all the sullen autumn sun they can.

Heirloom

I hold the women to the lamp:
slides grandfather kept in a shoebox.
A blonde wearing only cowboy boots
rides a fence, rough rock
sloping up behind her.
Then a brunette, one knee bent
in naked ease, leans against a rock wall,
her smile a faint reminder
of my mother's in her twenties.

The same two women sit
back to back in the next,
the camera closer in:
their skin is as smooth
as the boulders around them.
I picture my grandfather
at a late hour, flipping these nudes
on a white wall, his wife
somewhere asleep
or waiting up for him the way

you wait for me tonight,
quiet at corridor's end.
I hear the light turned out,
would join you, but a tiny projector
runs on even after the slides
are hid away.
As if I'd stared too long
at the sun, everywhere I look
rocks and women flash.

An Ascent in February

Grandfather was conceived beneath
a spruce: he remembers, he says,
the dark smell of evergreen
and where his mother sat
nursing him in the orchard
when blossoms haloed the trees.

When every branch bears a spine
of snow and sparrows grip old suet
swung in a gust, grandfather learns
what sweet fern is all over again.
Riding his father's neck, he'd known
the whole swamp: maple roots

coiled in moss, black pools,
the tree house with its tin roof.
Once a loud shelter from the rain,
only its nails were left, festering
the bark. And one mild midwinter day,
his back against the trunk,

grandfather fell asleep and dreamt
he lay on the sill of a dark house,
outside a room he knew was his;
and the quiet night covered him
with its shawl of cold sky.
Trying to rap on the glass,

he rolled off into deep snow.
He cried until his father's hands
took hold, then up and up and up
he climbed through the chill air
to where his mother stood waiting,
breathing perfect clouds in the porch light.

February

It is in this month that you dream
you're young again, the torn
muscle in your knee
all healed, and your stick
sends the puck careening
across the ice, past
fishing holes, beyond the reach
of the goalie guarding
the space between
two outcroppings on the shore.

The sun is not a burden,
you can look it
straight in the face,
and call out to your older brother to come
and see the pickerel
that's just entered the kingdom
of air and man and death,
and will be left behind
for fox or eagle.

And your skates are sharp again,
and you race end to end
in what seems a wink,
for dreams in February allow you
to ignore pesky things
like gravity and to jump
over barrels extending to the horizon,
which is turning
a lovely auburn,
color of your girl's hair
when you bury your eyes
behind her ear
and inhale and imagine
she is a cloud in human guise
and you have died but are actually
living harder than ever,
and the spruce overhead

calls to you
in squirrel chatter,

and the great rink fades,
and February has you pinned down
against its stiff pillow
of month-old snow,
and all is night,
and no dream calls you back
for the lucky break,
miraculous leap, prelude kiss,
at this end of time.

Nether

Nothing so literary as Dante or Dickens,
unrelated to flat lands in Europe
prone to flooding, this usage arrived in
paperback novels that made the rounds
in boarding school, passed from

boy to boy, so each of us learned
"nether" as an adjective applied
to lips, cheeks, regions, no mention
of worlds of damned or poor
surrounded by blast furnaces, though

Puncey Hall's basement conjured Hades.
All male, we dreamt of touching places
hidden on a woman's person while
hands sword-fought stiffies
into climaxes in bathroom stalls,

stifling our cries as we would later
in the nether world called marriage.
The word still stirs images of dark places
further darkened by skirts and underwear
below—there—where we yearned to explore,

ether and feather and never-never land.

The Crawler

"Historically, the genes that have been found in
worms have played an important role in humans as well."
—Dr. Pamela L. Larsen

I'd prefer to have someone,
ideally my father,
loading me to the chin,
my arms stuck straight out
like a forklift, but a
wobbly wheelbarrow
will have to serve to bear
logs across the lawn to shedside
where they can proceed
with their weathering.

Wood lifted from the bottom row
reveals a trove of bugs.
Stunned by the sudden sun,
they don't wait around to perform a song
as some spotlit entertainer might.
Millipedes slip into 50th gear
and disappear, two beetles head
for the hills—tufts of dead grass—
leaving behind

a magnificent night crawler,
pink-white, lightly moist,
plastic-looking in its perfection.
Laying the languorous worm the length of my hand
I dream of a record-size bass
yanking bobber down
to brown depths of pond,
a reverie that clings long after
I've returned the eyeless thing

to earth. As if it had sensed
its future inside a fish,
the crawler stretches long, then longer,
retracts, then squirms for dear life,
leaving me, hapless human,
to consider kinship,
the roles that fathers
and worms play
in the shaping of sinews,
of genes and world views.

In memory of John W. Little, 1919-1997

Eberhart on ESPN

> "Enigma rules, and the heart has no certainty."
> —Richard Eberhart, "Flux"

Searching the crowd for my father,
his red Eddie Bauer hat,
hoping for a close-up
of his never-grim visage taking in another
Dartmouth-Princeton pigskin encounter
on the Hanover plain—

I would be with him for the home opener
but have moved to downeast Maine,
tend two children and so rely
on the sports channel,
straining my eyes through
ranks of cheering alumni
for a glimpse of his patched jacket
and that Monsieur Hulot hat,
worn rain or shine—

A dozen autumn afternoons come back to me,
sitting with Dad and his class of '40 mates,
who never seemed to bring their children along,
leaving me stranded, obliged
to recount for the umpteenth time
my shaky job history, my need
for yet another graduate degree,
poetry contests almost won—

Then the camera singles out
a puffy, whiskered face above a body
bundled against October bleacher seats:
my God, it's Richard Eberhart,
poet emeritus of the Big Green!
He wears a lips-closed, enigmatic smile.
Does he know the ESPN cameraman aims at him?
That he beams on a national screen?

I can't help but think of his famous poem
"The Fury of Aerial Bombardment"
transposed this midday
to the Tigers' quarterback
completing a bomb,
which devastates the home crowd—

Such a wondrous face, with eyes
that must be as sensitive as a cat's,
so unlike those of the suddenly glum
men and women who surround him.
Bright-eyed and bushy-chinned
Eberhart stands in

for the father I never find
in the throng, whose red hat
I half-mock, half-admire
and now miss more than a grown man
or son should dare confess.

Calvin Trillin

I approach a man outside a restaurant in SoHo and ask him if he is Calvin Trillin. He says no. After I walk away, he turns to his friends and tells them that someone has asked him if he is Calvin Trillin. The group laughs; the man smiles, he is flattered, although he doesn't know that much about Trillin.

The next day, the man looks up Trillin in the card catalogue of the library and finds a few books. On the flaps there are photographs of Trillin, and the man realizes that he resembles the author very slightly. There is only a general resemblance, something as simple as a rounded face and dark hair. The man is very disappointed, but he checks out a book by Trillin, takes it home and reads it.

The man enjoys Trillin's writing. When he was young, the man had dreamed of becoming a writer, but the course of his life led him elsewhere. Now he studies Trillin's prose, becomes attached to the nuances of his style, and begins a journal. His wife, whose name happens to be Alice, looks askance, but lets it ride. She's got a life of her own; if her husband goes on the literary skids, she tells herself, she can get by.

Meanwhile, I fly back to Maine. I remember the encounter in front of the restaurant, mistaking a man for Trillin, and laugh at my idiocy. I did see Woody Allen later the same day, but didn't dare approach him. He was across the street, holding hands with his stepdaughter, who was looking in store windows. I was eating breakfast at the Greek place next door to Books & Company. One of the waiters pointed out Allen to me.

Soon the sun will rise over Central Park. We experience the dawn earlier, here on this island stretching out into the Gulf of Maine. Perhaps one day, we—myself, Calvin Trillin, Woody Allen, the man who was mistaken for Trillin—will get together on a higher plain. I doubt it. Ollam, I'm told, is the Hebrew word for crowd. We travel in different ollams.

Acknowledgments

Some of the poems collected here appeared previously in publications, sometimes in slightly different versions. The author extends thanks to editors: James Brasfield, George Van Deventer, Robert Farnsworth, Wendy Kindred, Constance Hunting, Gary Lawless, Phil Levin, Nan Lincoln, Stanley Lindberg, Steve Luttrell, Wesley McNair, Frederick Morgan, Carolyn Page, George Plimpton, Terry Plunkett, Roy Zarucchi, and the student editors at College of the Atlantic and the University of Southern Maine.

Bar Harbor Times: "Bathing Suit, ca. 1900," "To the Lady Who Sets Out Lawn Ornaments," "Car on a Lift," "Weeding Roses (The War)," "The Longing," "The Gymnasts," "February," "Somesville Invitation"
Black Fly Review: "At the Touch Tank"
The Café Review: "Springer on Chaise Lounge," "Cardiac Infarction"
Casco Bay Weekly: "Somes Harbor," "Vertigo of Tall Trees"
Columbia: "An Ascent in February"
Dartmouth Alumni Magazine: "Eberhart on ESPN"
Edge of Eden: "Ahab on a Whale Watch," "A Family of Four Acts Out 'Peter and the Wolf,'" "Possible Last Suppers," "The Man from U.N.C.L.E.," "The Crawler," "Desire Lines," "A Special Intelligence"
Georgia Review: "His Letters"
Hudson Review: "A Reminder," "The First Big Hit"
Journal of Friends of Acadia: "Ten Tourists Visit Baker's Island, Maine, ca. 1910"
Kennebec: "Ocean Drinker," "Facts of Catching," "The Red Nightshirt"
Maine in Print: "Young Pine"
Maine Progressive: "Heron on the Dam," "Death Toll Rises"
Maine Times: "The Sculptors," "Glacial Erotic," "Moose Head"
Nomad: "The Clearing," "Self Claim Area (La Guardia)"

Off the Coast: "Muse on I-95," "Tying His Son's Tie,"
"Backboard," "Frost Heaves"
Paris Review: "Running Out of Ideas One Day"
Potato Eyes: "Closing the House," "The Poetry Ken"
Puckerbrush Review: "When I Think of Elvers," "Swimming
Head:" "Marie Antoinette"
The Maine Weekly: "Winter Olympics Revisited"
Words & Images: "Calvin Trillin," "Watching the First
Pictures of Mars"

"Ten Tourists Visit Baker's Island, ca. 1900" won the 2002
Friends of Acadia poetry competition, judged by Marion
Stocking.
The poem "Heron on the Dam" appears in *The Breath of
Parted Lips: Voices from the Robert Frost Place*, volume II, edited by Sydney Lea (CavanKerry Press, 2003).
The poems "Glacial Erotic" and "Moose Head" appear in
The Maine Poets: A Verse Anthology, edited by Wesley
McNair (Down East Books, 2003).
"Weeding Roses (The War)" appeared in *The Maine
Organic Farmer & Gardener*, Autumn 2005.
Some of these poems originally appeared in *3,000 Dreams
Explained* (Nightshade Press, 1992).

Epigraphs:
Page (13): May Sarton, *Letters from Maine*. New York,
        W.W. Norton, 1997.
Page (39): Joseph Donahue, *World Well Broken*. Jersey
        City, New Jersey, Talisman House, 1995
Page (55): James Schuyler, *Selected Poems*. New York,
        Farrar Straus Giroux, 1988.
Page (73): David Graham, *Second Wind*. Texas Tech
        University Press, 1990.

Notes

p. 11, line 5: Michele Sanmicheli (ca. 1484-1559), Italian
      Renaissance architect and military engineer.

p. 16:   In the 1990s, the market in Maine for elvers—glass
      eels—exploded, driven largely by Japanese buyers.
      Seemingly overnight, fyke nets appeared
      strung across coves along the coast.

      line 15: "Somes Pond": see Elinor Wylie's poem
      "Atavism."

Page 19: The MDI Bio Lab is a marine and biomedical
      research facility located in Salisbury Cove, Maine.

Page 21: From Robert Desnos, *Chantefables et Chantefleurs*
      (Songfables and Songflowers), 1955. "The Lobster"
      and "The Pickerel" (page 79) first appeared in
      Translation, A Journal of Literary Translation and were
      reprinted as part of Backwoods Broadsides Chaplet
      Series Number 7, 1995, edited by Sylvester Pollet.

Page 26: line 1: Dale Chihuly (1941-), American glass
      artist.

Page 27: Epigraph from Tierney Thys, "Swimming Heads,"
      Natural History (August1994), 36-38.

Page 29: Rachel Field (1894-1943), novelist, poet, play-
      wright and author of children's books. Her "biogra-
      phical novel" *God's Pocket*, 1934, was reprinted in
      1999 by the Northeast Harbor Library. She had a
      home on Sutton Island, one of the five Cranberry
      Isles.
      line 30: *Beautiful Dreamer* was one of the last songs
      composed by Stephen Foster.

Page 34: Inspired by novelty book *3,000 Dreams Explained* by Madame Aspasia.

Page 42, line 6: "MOFGA": Maine Organic Farmers & Gardeners Association

line 21: "midden": a mound (such as a Native American shell heap) marking the site of early human habitation

Page 44, lines 4-6: "Shall I compare thee"—from William Shakespeare's eighteenth sonnet. "I wanna be your lover, baby"—from The Beatles' "I Wanna Be Your Man" (1963)

Page 45, line 11: "and a girl, my lord, in a flatbed Ford": from Eagles' song "Take It Easy."

Page 49, line 20: "cunnin'": cute, as in "The Cunnin' Little Thing" by Eugene Field.

Page 53, line 12: Horn & Hardart, a popular automat (self-service café) serving good dishes cheaply.

Page 61, lines 20-24: Auguste Rodin (1840-1917), French sculptor; Henry Moore (1898-1986), British sculptor; George Segal (1924-2000), American sculptor.

Page 64, line 17: "The Little Prince": from the book of the same name by Antoine de Saint-Exupéry.

line 32: "Norumbega": Some European explorers, with the help of Native Americans, believed that Norumbega, the lost city of gold, could be found where Bangor is now located.

Page 66: U.N.C.L.E. stands for United Network Command for Law Enforcement.

Page 67, lines 9-15: "I'm Dressing Myself," Young Peoples Records release, ca. 1950, sung by Artie Malvin and Lois Winters.

line 21: "lost forever on a mountain in Maine": paraphrase of title of Donn Fendler's *Lost on a Mountain in Maine*

Page 69, line 26: "Chiller Theatre," Saturday night horror movie show program on WPIX (Channel 11) in New York City in the 1970s and early '80s.

Page 71: Dr. Linda Austin hosted a national broadcast radio call-in show, "What's On Your Mind?"

Page 72, line 1: Eadweard Muybridge (1830-1904), British-born photographer, author of *Attitudes of Animals in Motion* (1881)

line13: Salt Pond Bay, part of Virgin Islands National Park on St. John

Page 79, line 2-3: "It's Istanbul, not Constantinople": from the popular song "Istanbul (Not Constantinople)" (1953), words by Jimmy Kennedy, music by Nat Simon.

Page 92: Epigraph from Richard Eberhart, *Selected Poems 1930-1965* (New York: New Directions, 1965).

Line 2: Eddie Bauer, "your source for casual, comfortable apparel and gear"

Line 14: Monsieur Hulot, French film character portrayed by Jacques Tati.

Page 90: Dr. Pamela Larsen, microbiologist.